STORIES OF BIBLE TIMES

HANNAH'S MARKET DAY

Written and illustrated by

ANNE FARNCOMBE

LUTTERWORTH PRESS – GUILDFORD AND LONDON

First published in Great Britain 1979

Other titles in this series

Biblical quotations are taken from the New English Bible (second edition) by kind permission of the Oxford and Cambridge University Presses

ISBN 0 7188 2359 1

Copyright © Lutterworth Press 1979

Printed in Hong Kong by
Colorcraft Ltd.

HANNAH SAT in the sand, sifting it through her fingers. She wondered if the other children would come to play with her. There was Simeon, whose father sold fruit in the market, and Mark, whose father made sandals and leather belts at his little stall. Ruth and Joseph might come, too, but they weren't in Jerusalem very often. Their father was a fisherman from Galilee, who salted the fish he caught so that it was fresh enough to sell when he made the journey down to Jerusalem. Hannah came to the market nearly every day, after she had fed the chickens and filled the water jars at home. She liked to be near Father as he stood beside his stall, and she loved to help arrange the gold jewellery and metal trinkets he sold.

She looked round. Father was bargaining with a man for the price of a gold necklace.

'Fifteen shekels,' said Father firmly.

'I'll give you ten,' said the man.

'Make it fourteen.'

'I won't pay more than twelve.'

Twelve shekels was the price settled upon. The customer paid the money; Father took it cheerfully and handed over the jewellery.

'Come and buy my wine jars!' called the man from the next stall. 'I made them myself, they're all good!'

'Fresh fruit and vegetables!' called another, and Hannah recognized Simeon's father. Simeon was there, unloading figs on to his father's stall. Hannah hurried over to join him.

'Shall I help?' she asked. Simeon gave her a sack of pomegranates.

'They can go in front,' he said. 'Just open the sack so that people can see the fruit.'

Hannah dragged the sack to the front of the stall. She was glad she wouldn't have to lift it up to tip the pomegranates out. She picked one out and examined it. It was just like a pinkish ball.

'You can eat one if you like,' said Simeon. 'Father always gives me some for my lunch.'

Hannah cut the hard ball open with Simeon's knife, and prised the fruit open. It was full of red juicy seeds which crunched as she ate them. It was certainly refreshing.

'Has your father got anything really valuable today?' asked Simeon.

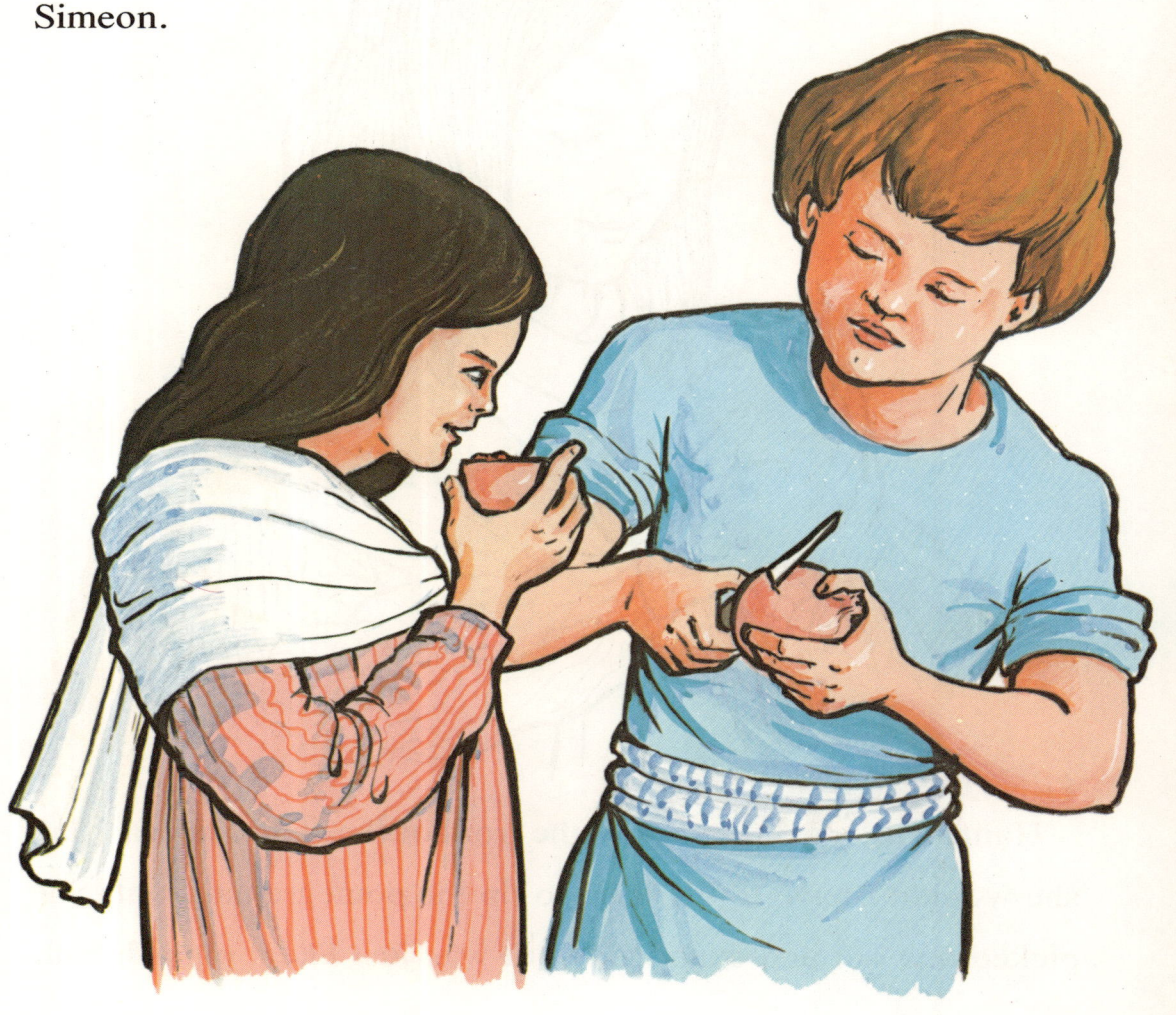

'He's just sold a gold necklace,' said Hannah. 'He met some travelling merchants the other day. They were taking some gold pieces to Syria to sell them there. Father noticed the gold necklace and offered to buy it for some silver. Now he's sold it

for more than he gave.'

'Has he got any mother-of-pearl?' asked Simeon. 'My father wants a piece to give to my cousin who's getting married.'

'He's got plenty,' said Hannah proudly. 'He went down to the Dead Sea yesterday and bought some there. That's where it comes from, you know.'

They ran back towards her father's stall. The sun was hot, and Father had put up a piece of cotton material to provide a little shade. It was always hot in the market, and there was always so

much noise — tin rattling, pottery being kicked or knocked giving a hollow clatter, and there was always the *bang! bang!* of hammers on leather or metal.

Hannah and Simeon collected Mark as they ran past his stall. He had just finished threading leather thongs through a pair of newly-made sandals.

'I'm not needed for a bit,' he said to Hannah. 'It will be a little while before Father finishes the next pair. Then I must go back to help.'

Everywhere people shouted, calling customers to buy, and holding out the goods they had to sell. Here and there foreign merchants stood with sacks of apples from Crete, or small

bottles of perfume from far off Arabia. One man showed off fine lengths of silk, and another spread baskets of all shapes and sizes round him. Hannah guessed that these had probably come all the way from Egypt.

Really, the market was the most exciting place to be in; there were the bright colours, the noise, and the smells — beautiful

rosewood and fragrant herbs, or the earthy smell of clay as it spun on the potter's wheel. Then there was the smell of animals, and cheese, and fish; of oil, and perfume, and wine. Women walked between the stalls, trying to exchange woven skirts, or head-dresses that they had made, for measures of wheat or olive oil.

Hannah's father sat at the back of the stall in the shade, while his little grey donkey nodded lazily in the sunshine.

'What have you sold?' Hannah asked, wondering if the little gold bracelet she loved had gone. There were more necklaces, too, some made with cheap clay beads, and others made of metal or glass. She liked them all, and was

always sad when one of her favourites was sold.

'Most people seem to be buying only food today,' said her father. 'Not many people are rich enough to buy the gold ornaments or metal bangles.'

Hannah, Simeon and Mark decided to play weddings. 'I'll be the bride,' said Hannah, 'and Simeon can be the bridegroom. Can I borrow this necklace for a little while, Father?' She picked up a gold coloured chain with little coins fixed to it. 'I promise I won't lose it!'

She fastened it round her head and pulled her head-dress up like Mother did. 'You must have a garland,' she said to Simeon, and raced to a patch of grass. 'There are some flowers here; we'll string these together,' she said. 'And this bush is beautiful — we'll take some flowers from this as well.'

'I'll go and get my flute,' said Mark, and disappeared to find his father's stall.

Together Hannah and Simeon walked slowly back to the market. They both felt they looked beautiful, and wondered if

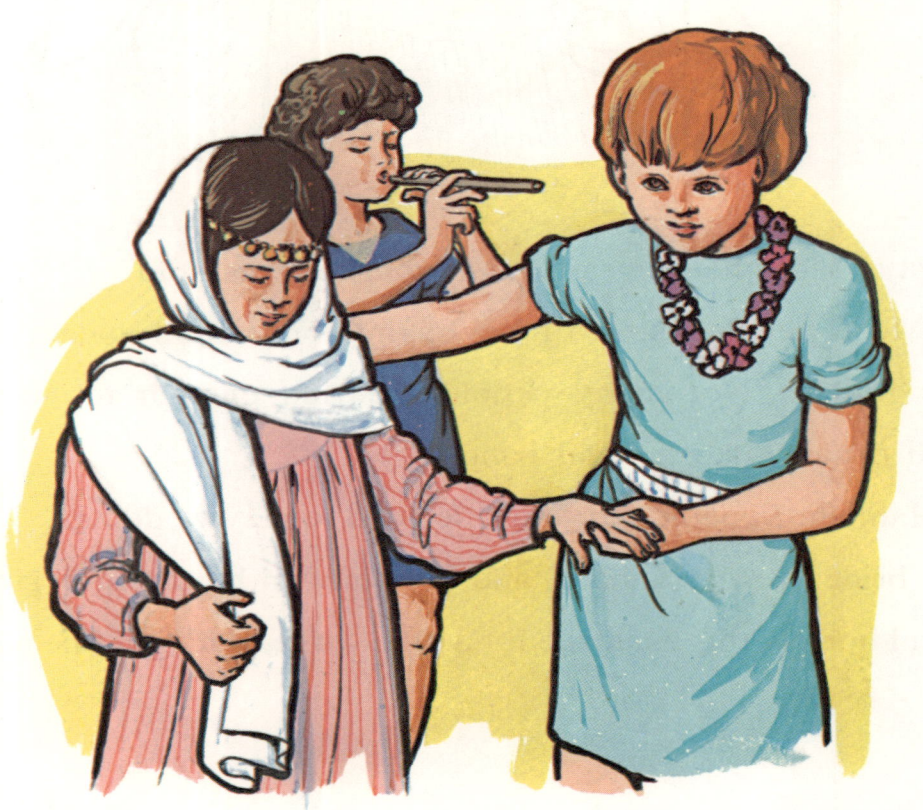

the people were admiring them. Mark began to play his flute and they danced to his music. Several people stopped to watch, tapping their feet. Just then Ruth and Joseph, the fisherman's children, hurried along.

'We're here!' they shouted, and joined the bride and groom, clapping their hands as they danced.

'Hannah! Where's my Hannah?'

'That's Father!' said Hannah. 'I wonder what he wants.' She ran off towards his stall, her gold coins tinkling and her headdress falling round her shoulders.

'Hannah! Come here quickly!' said her father as she pushed past the jars of wine and sacks of barley. A rich man stood in front of her father's stall.

'Come here and look at this!' said Father. 'Have you ever

seen anything like it?'

The rich man opened his hand. On a square of purple silk lay a large pearl, milky white and gleaming. It was the biggest pearl Hannah had ever seen. Father had a few small ones, at home, which he treasured, and which had cost him a lot of money. She

wondered if he was going to buy this one.

'It's just what I've always wanted,' her father sighed. 'But where am I going to find the money? It's terribly expensive!'

He turned out his leather money bag. Twelve . . . eighteen . . . twenty-two shekels. He took the gold coins from Hannah's head. 'You can have these, too, and these silver chains; and there are three gold bracelets here, and several pieces of mother-of-pearl.

Take them — and the money.'

The rich man laughed. 'That's not nearly enough,' he said. 'This pearl is worth far more than everything on this stall!'

'I'm collecting pearls,' said Hannah's father, 'and I need that one, I really do.' He put his hand to his head, smoothing his worried frown, and thought hard.

'Run home and get my other pearls,' he said at last to Hannah. 'Perhaps they would just make up the price.'

When Hannah came back they had settled everything. Father could have the huge precious pearl if he gave the rich man everything he had — all the expensive jewellery on his stall, his

collection of smaller pearls, and his little donkey.

'You won't have anything left!' said Hannah in dismay.

'Some things are so precious that it's worth giving up everything else for them,' explained her father as they walked home. He took out the pearl. It lay there, reflecting the sun, smooth and white and hard. It was quite beautiful.

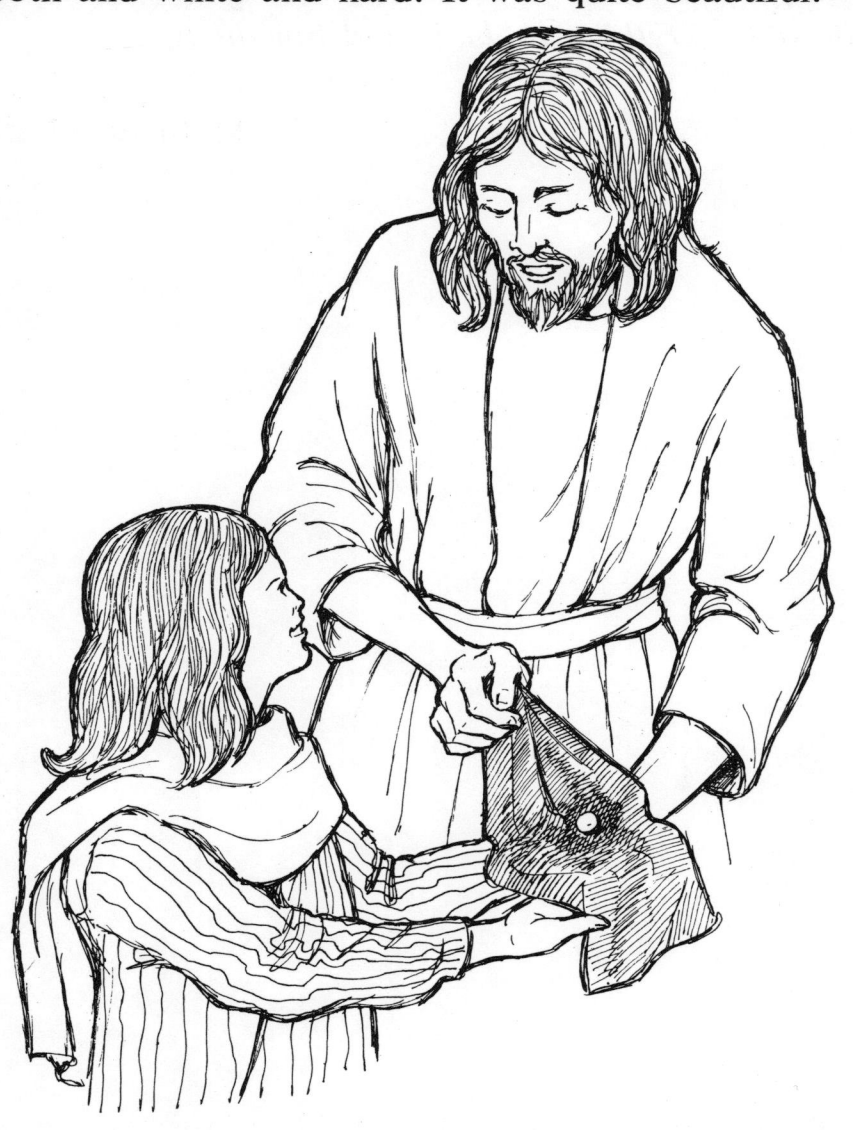

'Here is another picture of the kingdom of Heaven. A merchant looking out for fine pearls found one of very special value; so he went and sold everything he had, and bought it.'

Matthew 13:45–46